# BUSY IZZY

## and
## The Key to Lasting Joy

# BUSY IZZY
## and
## The Key to Lasting Joy

### Shayana Oakley
Illustrated By: Ishika Sharma

Published by Victorious You Press™ Charlotte NC, USA Copyright © 2023 Shayana Oakley All rights reserved.

No part of this book may be reproduced, distributed, or transmitted in any form by any means, without permission in writing from the author except in the case of reprints in the context of reviews, quotes, or references.

TITLE: Busy Izzy and The Key to Lasting Joy
First Printed: 2023
Illustrator: Ishika Sharma
ISBN: 978-1-959719-01-4 ISBN: (eBook) 978-1-959719-00-7
Library of Congress Control Number: 2023901540

Printed in the United States of America
www.victoriousyoupress.com

# Dedication

To my Busy Izzy and all the other busy bees in the world.
Keep buzzing your light all around.

TO: _____

FROM: _____

Busy Izzy was a boy,
who found the key to lasting
JOY!

He ran and jumped and hopped and skipped.

He taught the other kids his tricks.

Whenever it was bright and sunny,
he'd show the neighbors how he's so funny.

On days when rain kept him inside, he never cried or wondered why.

Instead, he turned the music on and got his family to dance along.

At school, he was cool, making him so smooth,
and his friends followed his every move.

Even teachers knew when to put down the chalk, because when Izzy starts talking...he'll talk, talk, talk!

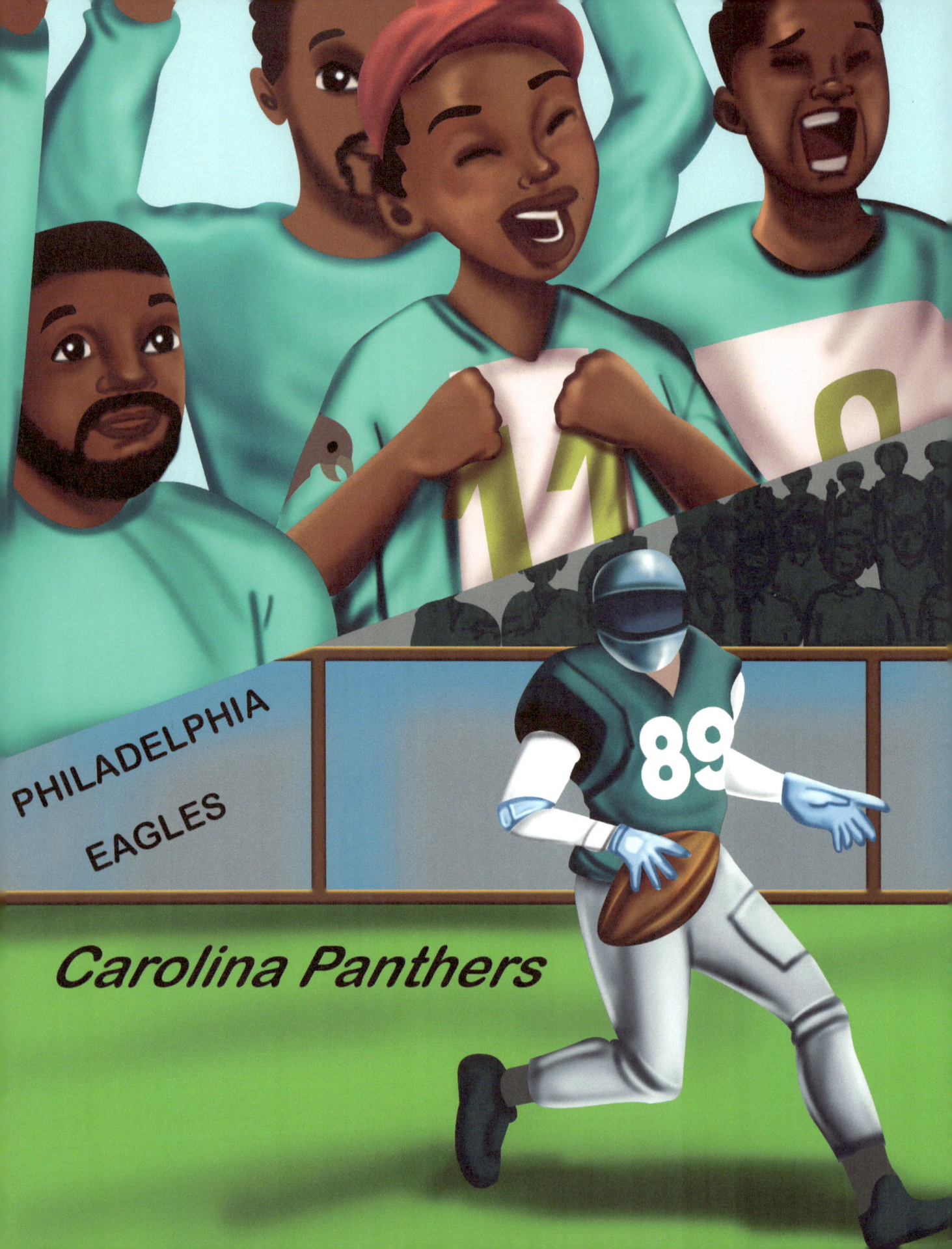

The weekends were his biggest glory.

He had adventures for days and told all the stories.

Like the time he went to the pro football game...

and drove around the Nascar Hall of Fame!

Every moment of life Izzy made sure to live
and inspired others with all his love to give.

You see, that was it! That's what Izzy found was "IT!"

When you give love you get love, just like this young boy because THAT is the key to lasting JOY!

# ABOUT THE AUTHOR

Shayana Oakley, also known as *TouShay*, is a Jamaican-American author with a passion for children's advocacy. She has worked with young people in many sectors, including public schools and behavioral health centers. Her mission has been consistent, in encouraging children to live the life of their dreams. The *Busy Izzy* series is based on her son Izzy, who is every bit of the word "busy." Oakley combines her love of rapping with her son's knack for adventure and brings a vibrant journey that will inspire any child.

Connect with Shayana at www.TouShay.net or vibes@toushay.net

Ingram Content Group UK Ltd.
Milton Keynes UK
UKHW051949140423
420144UK00003B/29